2

13

11

Puppy
Care

HOW TO LOOK
AFTER YOUR PET

Puppy
Care

How to Look
After Your Pet

Kim Dennis-Bryan

LONDON, NEW YORK, MUNICH, MELBOURNE, AND DELHI

WRITTEN AND EDITED BY Kim Dennis-Bryan FZS

CONSULTANTS Julius Neuman BVSc (Hons), MRCVS;
Menas Beaca DVM, MRCVS, & Lisa Guiney VN,
of The Mayhew Animal Home and Humane
Education Centre, London

ORIGINAL SERIES STYLING Lisa Lanzarini

DESIGNERS Cathy Tincknell and Lynne Moulding

DTP DESIGNER Dean Scholey

PUBLISHING MANAGER Cynthia O'Neill Collins

ART DIRECTOR Mark Richards

CATEGORY PUBLISHER Alex Kirkham

PRODUCTION Claire Pearson

First published in Great Britain in 2004 by
Dorling Kindersley Limited,
80 Strand, London WC2R 0RL
A Penguin Company

04 05 06 07 08 10 9 8 7 6 5 4 3 2 1

A CIP catalogue record for
this book is available
from the British Library.

ISBN 1-4053-0541-X

Reproduced by Colourscan, Singapore
Printed and bound at L.E.G.O. Italy

Discover more at
www.dk.com

Contents

Introduction

Your dog will be your best friend all his life. Make sure you look after him.

EVERYONE LOVES PUPPIES. These little animals are friendly and playful, and enjoy life to the full from the moment they wake until they fall asleep again. Puppies depend on us for a proper education and exercise as well as affection, food, and a comfortable bed. Your actions and decisions will determine how your puppy grows up. Training him to be well-behaved and obedient is fun but takes time.

Think carefully

Having a pet requires commitment from the whole family. You must decide if you have time to bond with, exercise, groom and train a puppy. Dogs vary a lot in size, so think about the space you have for a dog, too. Having a puppy is not a short-term commitment. A healthy dog lives 12 years or more, so you should think about the cost involved in keeping a dog over a long period.

All dogs need daily exercise. Do you have time to walk your dog every day?

WHICH TYPE OF DOG?

• Do you want a large or small breed? See (pp8–9 and p46.)

• Do you want a short-, wire-, or long-haired dog? (See pp26–27 and p46.)

• Do you want a purebred or mixed breed dog? See pp (8–9 and p46.)

Behavioural traits

All puppies have their own unique personalities, but purebred puppies behave in a more predictable way. Some purebreds are calmer, more friendly, and easier to train than other kinds. These qualities are more important than what a puppy looks like.

Most Labrador Retriever puppies make good family pets, growing up to be loyal, gentle, and eager to please.

Puppies with laid back personalities settle in quickly and will enjoy meeting your friends.

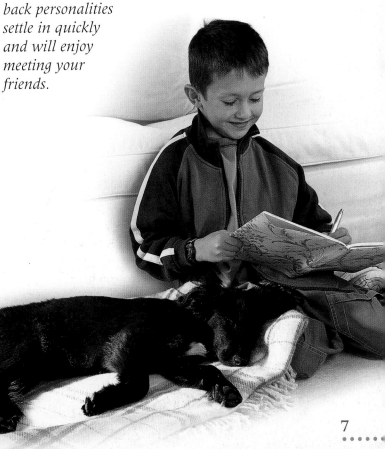

Family dogs

Dogs that are going to be part of a family should not be too large, too energetic, or too protective. They should be gentle and learn quickly how they must behave. These traits are seen in many herding and gun dogs. They make very popular pets.

Different dogs

Yorkshire Terriers are a type of toy dog.

DOGS COME IN ALL SHAPES and sizes – there are over 190 types, or breeds, known around the world! Each breed is different, and needs different amounts of exercise, space, food, grooming, and love. So before you choose a puppy, learn about the breeds you are interested in, to help you choose the dog that suits your family best.

Dog breeds

Dogs that look alike come from the same breed and are called purebreds. They usually have predictable needs and personalities. Breeds are divided into seven main groups. They are shown here.

Learning about breeds will help you choose the right puppy for you.

Toy dogs

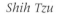

This Shih Tzu is one of the tiny breeds known as toy dogs. They are full of personality and may bark a lot! Toy dogs don't need lots of walking.

Shih Tzu

Beagle

Hounds

Hounds were bred to be hunters and have a built-in desire to chase things. They can be harder to train than other breeds and are not ideal pets for first-time owners.

West Highland White

Terriers

Breeds in the terrier group are tough and have strong personalities. They can be very lively and even aggressive. Most terriers are small or medium sized.

Rough Collie

Gundogs

This group includes the Labrador Retriever, the Golden Retriever, and most spaniels. Many breeds in this group are relaxed and easy to train. They are good with children and are popular family pets.

Cocker Spaniel

Herding dogs

This group contains the collies and cattle dogs. They are intelligent breeds with lots of energy. This makes them easy to train. Herding dogs need lots to do, or they will get bored.

German Shepherd Dog

Utility dogs

This contains all those breeds that don't fit into any other group! The Poodle is part of this varied group.

Poodle

Working dogs

Working dogs often make better guard dogs than family pets as they can be protective. The German Shepherd is a well known breed in this group.

Mixed breed dogs come in all shapes and sizes!

Mixed breed dogs

Some dogs are a mix of two or more breeds. Many mixed breed dogs make loving, happy pets. They are usually healthier than purebreds. It is harder to predict how they will grow up or how easy they will be to train.

Early life

Puppies learn as they play together.

WHEN A PUPPY IS BORN, her eyes are closed and she can't hear. She's helpless. For the first few weeks of her life, her mother gives her all the milk, love, and care she needs. By the age of six weeks or so, a puppy will be much more independent. Most puppies are ready to leave their mothers and go to new homes when they are seven or nine weeks old.

HELPING HAND

Sometimes a mother dog has so many puppies that she can't give them all enough milk. If this happens, some puppies need to be bottle fed. The owner helps the mother dog by giving the smaller puppies a special milk substitute from a baby's bottle.

Growing up

Puppies grow up much more quickly than human babies. At four weeks, they can run about and play. At five weeks, they have their first teeth! By about six months, they are almost fully-grown.

Puppies snuggle up to each other for warmth.

HOW A PUPPY GROWS, FROM ONE TO NINE WEEKS

One week old

The new puppy sleeps most of the time. She drinks milk from her mother if she is hungry.

Two weeks old

The puppy opens her eyes. It takes another week for her to see and hear properly.

Three weeks old

The puppy starts to explore the world around her. She still needs plenty of sleep.

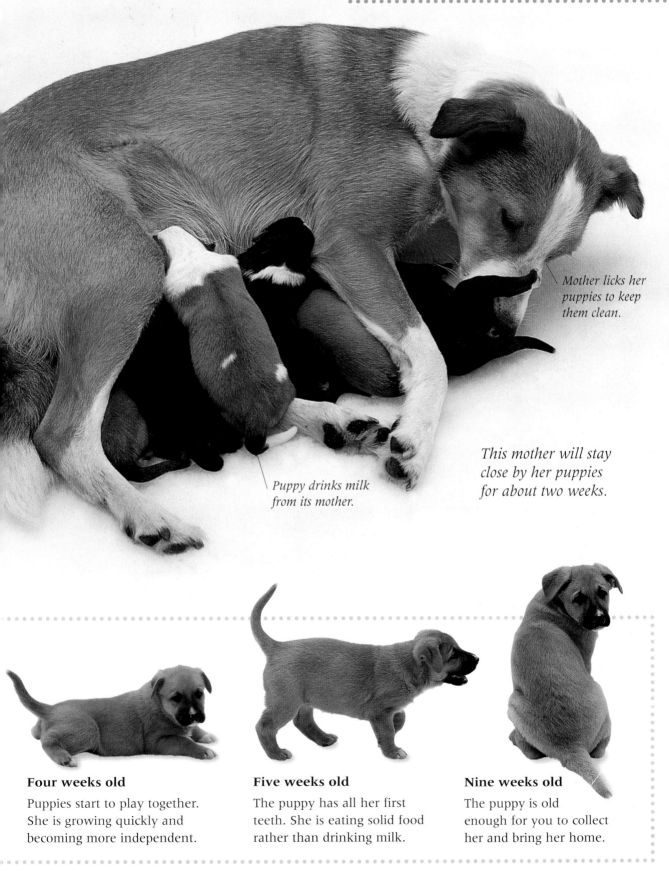

Mother licks her puppies to keep them clean.

Puppy drinks milk from its mother.

This mother will stay close by her puppies for about two weeks.

Four weeks old

Puppies start to play together. She is growing quickly and becoming more independent.

Five weeks old

The puppy has all her first teeth. She is eating solid food rather than drinking milk.

Nine weeks old

The puppy is old enough for you to collect her and bring her home.

11

Finding a puppy

THERE ARE LOTS OF WAYS to find a new puppy. If you would like a purebred dog, ask the local vet for help, and contact the breed club for a list of recommended breeders with puppies for sale. The vet may also know of some mixed breed puppies looking for a home. You can also phone the local animal shelter or dog charity. They often need to find homes for unwanted puppies.

Purebred pups, such as these Australian Sheep Dogs, cost a lot more than mixed breed puppies.

Purebred puppies

You can usually visit a breeder to look at a litter of puppies when the litter is about four weeks old. (You can't take the puppy you choose home until he is around nine weeks old.) Watch the mother of the puppies and see if she behaves in a nice way. Her puppies may grow up to be just like her.

Watch your puppy with her brothers and sisters to see how she behaves around other dogs.

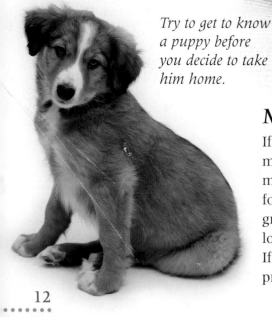

Try to get to know a puppy before you decide to take him home.

Mixed breed

If you would like to own a mixed breed puppy, try to meet one of his parents too, for an idea of how big he will grow. If you can't do this, look at the puppy's paws. If he has big paws, he will probably grow into a big dog.

PUPPY FARMS

Avoid buying a puppy from a puppy farm. These are places where large numbers of puppies are bred purely for profit. The puppies can be unhealthy, and may have behavioural problems.

A healthy puppy

You can tell a lot about your puppy's personality and health at your first meeting. She should be lively and friendly, with a clean coat, even under her tail near her bottom. (Remember to ask your vet to check your puppy's health, once you bring the pup home.)

Your puppy should have bright eyes

1 Check your puppy's nose is cool and damp when you touch it and, like the eyes, has no runny discharge.

2 Check her ears for black ear wax, which is a sign of mites. Mites can be easily treated. Ask your vet's advice.

3 Check her coat for evidence of fleas. Like ear mites, they are easily treated, using the correct products.

4 Check your puppy's feet. She should have five toes on the front paws, and four toes on the back paws.

13

Pet shops sell safe puppy toys, which your puppy can't swallow whole or chew bits off. Don't give your puppy your own old toys.

Getting ready

IT IS A BIG CHANGE for your puppy when he leaves his mother. You can help him settle into his new home by getting everything ready before he arrives. Buy the things you will need to look after him, and make sure your home is a safe place for a puppy to play. Puppies don't like lots of change all at once, so if you can buy the food that he is used to eating, he will be happier.

Safety

When your puppy explores your home he might want to chew things. Take a look around each room first, and put things that could hurt him out of his reach. Keep poisonous cleaning fluids in a locked cupboard. Don't leave sharp knives, scissors, or small objects like buttons lying around.

SAFETY TIPS

- Unplug electrical goods in case your puppy tries to chew the cables and gets a deadly shock.
- Put rubbish in puppy-proof bins.
- Cover up garden ponds while your puppy is small.
- Don't let your puppy eat house plants. They might make him sick.
- Lock garden gates so your puppy can't get out.

Busy times

Sometimes you will need to do chores without your puppy getting in your way. While you are busy, keep him in a crate or behind a baby's stairgate so he can't get into trouble. Choose a quiet place to put the crate, where your puppy can see you. Give him toys, water to drink, and a blanket to sit on. Put some newspaper in the crate in case he has an accident.

A baby's stairgate is a good way of keeping puppies out of trouble.

What to buy

You should buy your puppy a bed, puppy food, a bowl for food, a different bowl for water, toys, a collar with an name tag, and a lead. You will also need cleaning liquids and old newspapers to use until your puppy is housetrained.

Separate water and food bowls

Puppy food

Toys and chews

Nylon or leather collar, with identity tag

A lead for walks

Old newspaper

Cleaning materials

Line your puppy's bed with a cosy blanket.

A puppy chew will help your puppy's teeth.

Coming home

YOU'LL BE VERY EXCITED when it is time to collect your new pet. It's a big day for you, but it's an even bigger one for your puppy. He will be leaving his mother, brothers and sisters, and everything he knows, and he might get upset or worried on the journey. If this happens, you can help him if you keep calm and quiet. Talk to your puppy in a gentle voice, and let him know that everything will be alright.

Confident puppies generally accept change very easily.

Travelling

Bring your puppy home in a large cardboard box or a puppy crate, lined with newspaper and a blanket. If it is the first time that your puppy has been in a car, he might be travel-sick. Don't worry about this. Regular, short trips should get him used to car journeys.

Pet carrier with air holes in the sides

You can buy pet carriers at most pet shops.

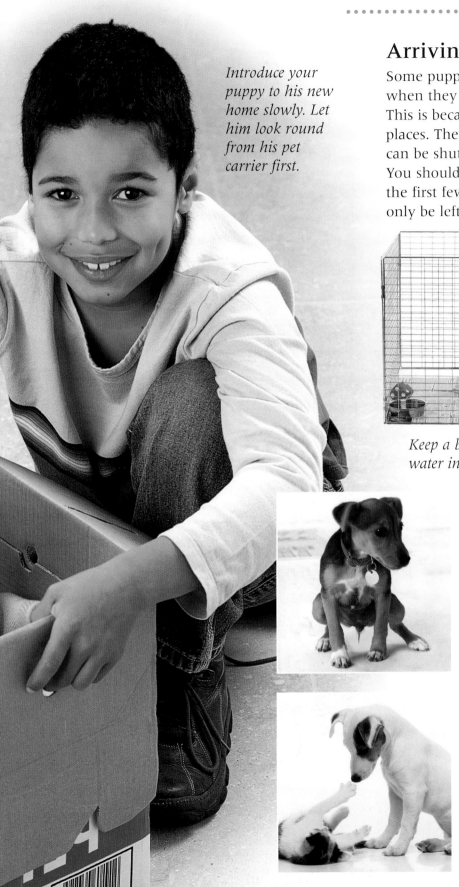

Introduce your puppy to his new home slowly. Let him look round from his pet carrier first.

Arriving home

Some puppies are put in puppy pens when they first get to their new homes. This is because they feel safer in small places. They eat and sleep there, and can be shut in if you need to go out. You shouldn't leave a puppy alone for the first few days. After that, he should only be left for a few hours at any time.

Keep a bowl of fresh drinking water in your puppy's pen.

Toilet stop

As soon as you get home, put your puppy in the garden or on newspaper to relieve himself. Look pleased and say "Well done" if he does the right thing. There are bound to be a few accidents at first.

Other pets

Other pets in your home might be jealous of the new puppy. Introduce them to your new dog carefully. Watch over their first few meetings and make sure your pets play nicely and don't fight.

17

Feeding

TO KEEP HEALTHY, your puppy needs to eat the right amount of the right food, at regular times. Give her specially-made puppy food and not dog food. Your vet, or the breeder, can give you a diet sheet that shows what she should eat, depending on her age. Make any changes to her diet bit by bit, so she has time to get used to them.

Small puppies have small stomachs, so they eat little and often.

What to feed

There are three main kinds of puppy food. A 'complete' food contains everything a puppy needs, so you won't have to add anything. It can be wet or dry and is easy to store. Or you might want to feed your puppy tinned or fresh meat. You should mix these foods with puppy biscuit, to give her a balanced diet.

Complete wet food

Complete dried food

Chicken meat with puppy biscuit

1 Be careful with hygiene when you prepare your puppy's meal. Put her food bowl on some kitchen paper so it doesn't touch the kitchen work tops.

2 Your puppy should not be possessive about her food or rush to eat it. To prevent this happening, offer her a tit-bit before letting her eat.

18

HOW MANY MEALS?

Age	Meals per day
8–12 weeks	4 meals
13–16 weeks	3 meals
6 months	2 meals
10 months	2 meals (small breeds); 1 main meal and one smaller one (large breeds)

Cleaning up

After your puppy has finished eating, wash her food bowl. This is a good time to wash and refill her water bowl, too.

After feeding a tit-bit to your puppy, wash your hands.

RULES OF FEEDING

1. Set regular meal times.

2. Make sure your puppy always has a bowl of fresh water to drink.

3. Give your pet puppy food, not dog food. Puppies need different diets to adult dogs.

4. Weigh your puppy every week to find out how much food you need to feed her.

5. Don't make sudden changes to a puppy's diet. Do it slowly.

6. Don't give your dog too much to eat. Fat dogs do not live as long as fit, sleek dogs.

7. Don't give your puppy cow's milk to drink.

8. Give your puppy proper dog treats as a reward for doing the right thing. But not too often!

8. Never give your puppy chocolate.

3 You should then be welcome when your dog eats as she will see you as the person who gives her food. Never approach your puppy from behind while she is eating as this may surprise her.

Meet the vet

YOU SHOULD TAKE YOUR PUPPY to the vet the day after you bring him home. The vet will check the puppy and give him the jabs your pet needs to keep well. It's a good idea to sign up with a vet close to home, so you can get there quickly in an emergency.

Bring your pet to the vet's in a pet carrier.

First appointment

Try to see the vet either at the beginning or end of surgery hours. This way your puppy won't meet other animals until he has been fully vaccinated.

1 The vet will look your puppy over carefully to check he is healthy. He will look at his eyes, ears, teeth, jaws, and coat, as well as feeling his tummy for swellings that shouldn't be there.

2 Your puppy might have long nails, as he hasn't had any walks to wear them down yet. If so, the vet will cut them back.

Reassure your puppy if he is worried by his first visit to the vet.

3 The vet will listen to your puppy's heart through a stethoscope, which makes his heart-beat easier to hear.

Protecting your puppy

Your vet will give your puppy injections to protect him from dangerous illnesses. The puppy has his first injection when he is between 8 and 12 weeks old. He has another at 14 to 16 weeks. Your puppy will be fully protected a week after the second injection.

RABIES

In some countries your puppy will need to have an injection to protect him against a serious illness called rabies. Your vet will know about this.

It is important to protect your puppy from disease.

Healthcare

YOUR VET knows a lot about puppies. He can tell you how to look after your puppy's health. He can answer any questions you might have, too. You will have to do some things every day, or every week, to look after your puppy. The vet can explain why these things matter, and show you and your parents exactly how to do them.

When you hold your pet, keep one arm under his bottom.

Identity chips are as small as a grain of rice.

Identity chipping

Your vet can help you keep your pet safe, by injecting a tiny chip into his neck. If your puppy gets lost, the chip can be scanned by the police. It tells them how to find you so they can return the puppy to you.

Worming tablet being given with dried food

Worming

You must 'worm' your puppy every three months to get rid of tiny worms in his tummy. The vet will give you the correct dosage based on your puppy's weight. Usually you'll mix a powder or pill into your pet's next meal.

Tooth and nail

Clean your puppy's teeth every day with a dog's toothbrush and animal toothpaste. Your vet can show you what to do. Clipping nails has to be done very carefully, because your puppy's nails will bleed if they are cut too short. Leave this job to your parents.

Small toothbrush

Finger toothbrush

Clippers

Clean the outside of your puppy's teeth.

Every day
- Feed your puppy.
- Fill up his water bowl.
- Brush his teeth.
- Practise training.
- Spend time with your puppy. Groom him, check his eyes and ears are clean, and his paws are not sore.

Every week
- Weigh your puppy to check he is getting the right amount of food for his size.
- Check his collar fits.

Other times
- Worm every three months
- Annual booster injections

Keeping records

Keep all your puppy's records in a file or folder. Store his vaccination certificate, photographs, and other papers inside. You should also write down when his next booster injections and worming tablets are due.

Vaccination certificate

File holding puppy's records

Settling in

Poodle puppy

Soft puppy toy being used as a comforter

Puppies learn quickly, so try to follow a routine from the start.

IT IS A GOOD IDEA TO teach your puppy your family's rules from the very beginning. She will need to know where she goes to the toilet, and where she eats and sleeps. She also needs to learn how to be alone. Your puppy might be upset at night when you and your family go to bed. If she starts to whine, don't go to her. She will fall asleep in the end. After a few days, she will get used to sleeping by herself.

Bedtime

Play with your puppy for a while before you go to bed. This will tire her out so she feels like sleeping. At night, leave the radio on so your puppy can hear voices and doesn't feel lonely. Put a warm hot-water bottle wrapped in a blanket in her crate, so she can snuggle against it.

FITTING A COLLAR

You should get your puppy used to her collar as soon as possible. Check that it fits properly. You should be able to get two fingers between the collar and your puppy's neck. She may scratch the collar at first, but will soon forget about it – especially if you distract her with a game!

Puppies often sniff around before and after going to the toilet.

Toilet-training

Teach your puppy where he is allowed to go to the toilet. Pick a place outside, and take him on a 'toilet-trip' there every two hours. He will need to go after food or a nap, too. Take him to the same place every time. Wait until he goes, even if it takes a few minutes. Then cuddle and praise him when he does the right thing.

Which name?

Choose a short name for your puppy, like Sadie or Star. Avoid names, such as Beau or Kit, that sound like command words. Use her name as often as you can. She will quickly get used to it and come when you call her.

1 To teach your puppy her name, sit or kneel on the floor with your arms out, and call to her in a friendly voice.

2 If she comes to you, show her you're pleased. Give your puppy a treat. (Later you can replace treats with cuddles).

3 By getting down with your puppy, you help her learn not to jump up. She is then less likely to do it as she gets bigger.

When your puppy knows her name, you can start to train her.

Grooming

Dogs with long fur need lots of grooming.

GROOM YOUR PUPPY every day. This will keep her coat soft, clean, and free of tangles. It is also a good time to check that there are no fleas or ticks in her fur, or mites or grass seeds in her ears. Finally, it helps you to teach your puppy that she must sit still sometimes, even if she wants to move about. This is an important lesson for a puppy.

Brush or comb?

There are lots of different grooming tools. Ask the breeder or the vet which type is best for your puppy's fur. Some dogs have unusual fur, such as Poodles with their curly coats. They may need to visit a grooming salon to keep their coats looking good.

Poodle fur needs special grooming care.

Comb

Pad

Brush

Daily brushing

If you brush your pet every day, you take away most of her loose hairs, and help keep your home tidy! Otherwise dogs can shed a lot of hair around your home, especially in the spring when they lose their thick winter fur.

Long, silky coats take time to comb.

BATHING

Try not to bath a puppy that is under 6 months old. If she is really dirty, rinse her with plain water. Dry mud will usually just brush out.

1 Get your puppy used to being groomed a little at a time. Stroke her until she settles down and then start to brush her gently. Always begin on the body.

2 Gradually move down her front and back legs to her feet. If the hair between her toes needs trimming, cut it carefully. Remember to use round-ended scissors.

3 Next brush her head and ears. The skin inside her ears is very delicate so brush and comb them gently. Finally, clean her eyes using a pet tissue.

Never use human shampoo on a puppy.

Wipe downwards away from the eye when cleaning it.

4 Your puppy may sleep after she has been groomed. This is because she is happy and feels totally relaxed.

Dog talk

THERE ARE LOTS OF WAYS that your puppy can tell you how he is feeling. He might bark when he wants something, or wag his tail when he's happy. If you learn to understand what your puppy is 'saying', it will help you when you start to train him.

Is your puppy panting? Then he feels hot!

Barking

Puppies bark when they are excited. They also bark to get your attention when they want to play or go out to the toilet. Older puppies bark if someone comes to the door or if they hear a strange sound. This is a warning bark. It's easy to tell the two barks apart.

Puppies hold their heads high when they bark.

A waggly tail

Your puppy's tail shows you how he is feeling. He wags his tail from side to side when he's happy or excited. If his tail is standing straight up, he's being very alert and aware. And when your puppy is sad, he'll curl his tail between his legs.

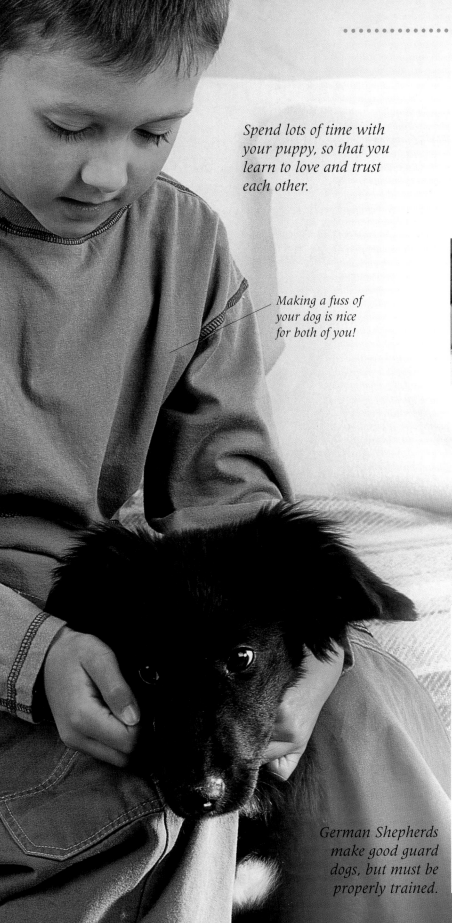

Spend lots of time with your puppy, so that you learn to love and trust each other.

Making a fuss of your dog is nice for both of you!

CHEWING

Does your puppy chew a lot? If she is under seven months, she is probably teething. If she chews things after that, she is doing it to learn about her surroundings. Give her lots of hide chews to bite on, so she won't chew the furniture!

Guard dogs

As puppies grow older, they start to protect their homes. They bark to warn you when a stranger comes to the door.

German Shepherds make good guard dogs, but must be properly trained.

29

Know your puppy

WILD DOGS LIVE IN FAMILY groups called packs. One dog is the leader. He makes sure the others follow the rules. All the dogs have a place in the pack, but some dogs are more dominant (more powerful) than others. When you get a dog, you and your family become his 'pack'. If he knows that your parents lead the pack, and understands his place, he will be happy to follow your rules.

When a puppy rolls over to have his tummy rubbed, he's also showing that he knows you are the boss!

Body language

A puppy uses his whole body to express himself. He will be bouncy when he's playing and sad if you scold him. He may spring to attention, for example, if he sees or hears another dog. The hairs, or 'hackles' along the middle of his his back may stand up. His ears, tail, and hair show his mood.

In a pack of Foxhounds, some dogs have higher status than other dogs.

The dominant puppy stands while the other rolls over.

Curled tail

Play-bow

If your puppy wants you to play with him, he will crouch down, with his bottom in the air. This is called a play-bow. Then he'll wag his tail and bark to get your attention.

The senses

A puppy hears and smells things better than a human can. She will know when there is someone at the door before the doorbell rings, and will prick up her ears to see if she knows who the caller is.

Ears beginning to prick up

Alert

An alert puppy will listen, and sniff the air. If she needs to investigate further, she will leap up for a closer look. She can spot movement more quickly than a human can, but she doesn't see colour in the same way.

Submissive body language

This puppy's pricked ears and fixed stare show she is alert.

Sad

If your puppy is naughty and you scold her, she will look sad, putting her ears down and her tail between her legs. She may also crouch down or roll over on her back to say sorry.

Making friends

ONE OF THE BEST things you can do for your puppy is teach her about the world around her. The most important time to do this is when she is aged between eight and twelve weeks. Introduce her to as many people, sights, and sounds as you can. Then she won't have any problems when she's older and goes out for walks.

The first person a puppy bonds with is her new owner.

Meeting the family

Your puppy may be easily scared at first, so introduce other family members and pets carefully. Ask everyone to sit on the floor. If your puppy goes up to them, they can make a fuss of her. Otherwise they should leave her alone to explore in her own time.

Puppies and kittens can become good friends.

CHECKLIST

• Never rush your puppy.

• Watch over your puppy when she meets other pets.

• Introduce your puppy to as many different people and situations as possible.

Puppy parties

Ask your vet if there are any 'puppy parties' in your area. They are a chance for you to introduce your puppy to other pets, so you can teach her how to behave with other dogs as well as people.

A puppy can go to puppy parties from the age of 12 weeks.

Your puppy should meet lots of different people.

Meeting people

Don't wait for a party to start introducing your puppy to new people. Ask your friends round to play. Carry her to the park, or down your street so she can meet your neighbours.

If your puppy is friendly, you can take her with you to all sorts of places!

Your puppy will meet strange dogs on her walks. These meetings should be friendly.

A friendly puppy

The more things your puppy does while she is young, the better. However, always make sure that she's enjoying herself. If she backs away from something, you may be rushing her. Slow down, and give your puppy more time. Don't fuss over her. She will discover things when she is ready.

Your puppy may not want to walk on a lead at first!

How to train

IT'S UP TO YOU to teach your puppy how to behave. Show your puppy what you want him to do, and reward him at once when he gets it right! Start training him straight away, just for a few minutes. It should be fun, but remember you are teaching your puppy, not playing a game. Be patient and don't give up!

Starting out

As well as toilet-training, teach your puppy his name first of all (see p25). He also needs to understand the word "no", so that you can stop him from getting into trouble. Always say "no" in a firm voice. Don't laugh, even if your puppy is doing something funny. Your puppy cannot understand human language, so try to make your body signals match your words.

Boy waves finger to back up saying "no"

PATIENCE

Always be patient with your puppy. Make sure the whole family uses the same words, such as "OK", when training her. Don't lose your temper when things go wrong. Never, ever hit your puppy.

Rewards

When your puppy does the right thing, praise or hug him straight away. He'll see that doing what you ask brings rewards! End training sessions on a good note, with something your puppy can do well.

Let your puppy play with his favourite toy after a good training session, to reward him.

Discipline

Sometimes you will have to punish your puppy for being naughty, or for biting hard when you are playing. Ignore your puppy and don't look at him. He'll know he has done something wrong and will quickly learn to stop it.

Be consistent with your puppy as this helps him to learn.

WAITING

Your puppy should stand or sit quietly while you prepare his food. He should also wait until you have put his dish down and moved away before he starts to eat. Follow this house rule from day one. Often all you need to do is ask your puppy to "wait" while you're putting out his food, then tell him "OK" in a firm voice.

Training

THE BEST AGE FOR TRAINING your puppy is between the age of three to six months. He will soon learn to do what you ask if you praise and reward him when he's good and show that you're disappointed with him if he's naughty. You can teach him to sit, lie down, and do other tricks. He also needs to learn how to behave on the lead when you go out for walks. If you want to do more with your puppy, find out if your local dog club runs an obedience class that you can go to.

Puppies are fast learners and eager to please.

Sitting

Teach your puppy to sit. Call his name to get his attention. When he is standing in front of you, show him a treat. Move it slowly back over his head. Your puppy will have to sit down so that he can keep watching the treat. At this point, say "sit" in a firm voice. When he sits down, show him you're pleased by giving him the treat and praising him.

Eventually your puppy will learn to do the right thing.

Your puppy might jump up for the treat instead of sitting! Keep calm and try again.

TRAINING TIP

Always say your puppy's name first to get his attention. Then give a command, such as "sit", in a firm but friendly voice.

Lying down

Ask your puppy to sit. Hold a treat under her nose, then move it down to the floor. Your puppy will follow the food with her nose. Move the treat forwards. As your puppy stretches out to reach it, say "down". Give her the treat and praise her when she's down.

Fetch

Puppies love to chase and fetch toys. Throw a toy for your puppy. As she runs after it say her name and "fetch" in a friendly voice. As she brings it back to you, hold out your hand, say her name, and ask her to "bring" the toy to you.

1 This puppy is learning to fetch toys but has yet to learn to bring them back.

2 Never chase your puppy if it refuses to give you a toy. You will be giving her the wrong signal. Instead of teaching her to fetch, she will think she is playing chase.

DOG CLUBS

Before joining a dog club, go along as a visitor one evening without your puppy to get an idea of what is involved.

First walks

Fasten the lead to your puppy before you go out so he can't run away.

IT'S AN EXCITING DAY when you take your puppy for his first walk. Remember there are dangers for a puppy outside, and it's up to you to keep him safe and under control. Don't let your puppy run off, especially near a road, and bear in mind that other people might not like dogs as much as you do.

Walking on a lead

Taking your puppy for walks is great fun as long as she behaves. If your puppy starts to pull, stand still. When she looks back to see why you have stopped, ask her to "come". Praise her for doing so, and walk backwards a few steps before continuing forwards. She will soon learn that she will reach the park sooner if she walks by your side rather than rushing ahead of you.

Walk to an open space where your puppy has plenty of room to play.

1 It's important to train your puppy to cross a road safely. Keep the lead short so she can't run too far ahead of you.

2 Your puppy must learn to sit and wait until the road is clear. Make sure she knows it's wrong to chase cyclists or cars.

3 When it is safe to cross, tell your puppy to walk on by your side. She should do this quietly and not rush forwards.

Drying off

If your puppy gets wet
during a walk, rub him
dry so that he doesn't
get cold. Be gentle
with his paws.

SCOOPING UP

Always carry a plastic
bag or pooper scooper
on your walk, so you
can clean up after your
puppy if he goes to the
toilet while you're out.

!

Children walking
with a puppy
should always be
accompanied by a
responsible adult.

Playing

PUPPIES LOVE TO PLAY. Playing teaches them about the world around them and helps to keep them fit and happy. Even young puppies enjoy games of fetch. Older puppies enjoy playing hide-and-seek with hidden toys, which they find using their great sense of smell.

A ball is a good toy for a puppy. Make sure it is quite large so your puppy can't swallow it.

Which toy?

There are lots of toys that you can buy for puppies. They love soft toys, strong rubber toys that they can chew and chew, or toys that make a squeaky noise. Whichever toys you choose for your dog, don't let her be possessive about them. Never give your puppy your old toys as they may not be safe for her to chew.

Rope toy

Squeaky soft toy

Tennis ball

Rubber bone

Ball with bumpy surface

Flavoured chews

PLAY-BITING

Puppies play-bite their brothers and sisters. Show your puppy it isn't okay to do it to you by stopping any game at once if she gets too excited or rough. She will soon learn to play more gently.

Tug-of-war

Your puppy will like playing tug-of-war, but it isn't a good game for her to learn. As puppies grow up they can get very strong. When she's a grown dog, she might pull you over in a game, which will be no fun at all.

Playtime

Puppies enjoy all sorts of games. They will chase after balls, retrieve soft toys, and search for hidden toys. If you give your puppy a new toy, he'll probably get very excited. However, he should always give it back to you if you ask him for it.

Rope toys are fun to chew and are good for games of fetch, too.

1 This puppy has a new toy. He wags his tail and pounces on it in excitement. He then finds out the toy squeaks.

2 Next he mouths and rolls on the toy. This marks it with his scent. He may also carry the toy around with him for awhile.

3 However much he likes his toy, he must give it up when you ask. Praise him so he knows he has done the right thing.

Illness

When a puppy feels unwell, he often looks sad. His nose may feel dry and warm rather than cool and wet.

AS YOU GET TO KNOW your puppy, you will see immediately when she is feeling ill. Until then, be careful, as young puppies can get sick very quickly. Luckily they usually get better just as fast and are soon back to normal, and wanting to play! If you think your puppy is seriously ill, take her to the vet at once.

Look for symptoms

A sick puppy looks sad, won't play, and sleeps more than usual. If your puppy won't eat, check she's still drinking as puppies get dehydrated quickly. If she's stretching a lot, she may have a tummy problem. If she is sick more than once, or has diarrhoea, it is also cause for concern, and so is not going to the toilet as usual. Phone the vet if you're worried.

TRAVELLING

If your puppy spends time in the car, be very careful. In hot weather puppies can get heatstroke and it is a serious condition. Never leave your puppy in a car for a long time, even with a window open. If you must leave her for more than a few minutes, make sure she has plenty of water to drink.

Ear and eye drops

One day you or your parents may need to give your puppy ear or eye drops. Be calm and quiet when you do this, to help keep your puppy relaxed. Speak reassuringly and give your puppy a hug afterwards.

Keep your puppy quiet and relaxed while you give him eardrops.

This puppy has an itch, but excessive scratching may be due to fleas.

Fleas

If your puppy is scratching more than usual, use a flea comb to check her for fleas. If you find fleas, treat the puppy promptly to avoid complications.

INSECT STINGS

If an insect bites or stings your puppy, it may cause a swelling. Sometimes these lumps appear on your puppy's face. A swelling on her nose or on her throat may make it hard for your puppy to breathe. To be safe, take her to the vet to rule out snake bite or an allergic reaction. The vet may give your puppy an injection. This will help to bring down the swelling.

Keep your sick puppy warm and comfortable as you travel to the vet surgery.

Puppy wrapped in a blanket to go to the vet

Emergencies

If your puppy is in pain, or bleeding from an injury, take her to the vet straight away. She may have a serious problem and any delay could be fatal. The pain may make your puppy feel cross, so take extra care travelling to the vets. Try to carry her in a crate, or a large box lined with a blanket, to avoid moving her about too much.

Growing up

YOUR PUPPY WILL GROW QUICKLY over her first year. In 'dog years', she is actually growing up about seven times faster than you are. Dogs can live for over 12 (human) years. Looking after an adult dog carries responsibilities for all your family to think about.

Most puppies reach full size by 6 months of age.

Neutering

During your first few months of puppy ownership, you will need to decide whether or not to have your puppy neutered. This operation will prevent your pet from having puppies of its own when it grows up. Female puppies mature at 6 to 8 months, male puppies at 8 to 12 months. Your vet can tell you about the operation and when it is best to carry it out.

Remember, if you let your female dog breed, you will have to find homes for all the puppies.

A change of diet

When your pet is fully grown, she will need to switch from puppy food to adult dog food. This change should be made slowly, over a few days, to prevent tummy upsets.

As your dog ages, you may have to change her diet again. Ask your vet's advice about this.

Do not overfeed your dog. Fat dogs are unhealthy.

As your puppy grows, check the fit of her collar and loosen it as necessary. She may need a new collar sometimes.

Puppies grow quickly. At seven weeks (see p25), this puppy barely reached the girl's knees. Now nine months old, she can easily reach her waist.

Dental care

Some puppies do not lose all their first teeth as they should. You may see the old teeth along with the new ones when you clean your puppy's teeth. Your vet can also check for them during a routine veterinary examination. First teeth that don't fall out on their own should be removed to prevent overcrowding.

GETTING OLDER

Older dogs do not walk as far as they once did because, like humans, they get stiff joints. They may also get a little deaf, something you should think about if they are off the lead. Older dogs may need a coat to keep them warm on cool days.

Dog breed facts

Welsh Terriers are medium-sized dogs.

THE TABLE BELOW shows the adult size of some of the more popular dog breeds. It also gives an idea of the amount of grooming and exercise each breed of dog needs. For further information, you can look at various web sites (see below).

Recommended web sites
www.the-kennel-club.org.uk
www.akc.org

KEY

Up to 30 cm	little
30–55 cm	moderate
Over 55 cm	substantial

The silhouettes show the average height of a ten-year-old child and the adult height of a small, medium and large dog.

150 cm/
60 ins

120cm/
48 ins

90 cm/
36i ns

60 cm/
24 ins

30 cm/
12 ins

BREED	SIZE	AMOUNT OF EXERCISE	AMOUNT OF GROOMING
Chihuahua (short coat)			
Chihuahua (long coat)			
Yorkshire Terrier			
Australian Silky Terrier			
Maltese Terrier			
Shih Tzu			
Dachshund (smooth coat)			
Dachshund (long coat)			
Dachshund (wire coat)			
Toy Poodle			
West Highland White			
Cavalier King Charles			
Poodle (Mini/Standard)			
Cocker Spaniel			
Australian Cattle Dog			
English Springer Spaniel			
Beagle			
Staffordshire Bull Terrier			
Border Collie			
Labrador Retriever			
Golden Retriever			
German Shepherd Dog			
Boxer			
Rough Collie			
Dobermann			

Index

Acknowledgements

Dorling Kindersley would like to thank:
The Mayhew Animal Home for Benjy the mixed breed puppy;
the Richbourne Kennels for Star, Buttons, and Fliss the
Labrador Retriever puppies;
Suzanne and Molly, her Hungarian Vizla puppy;
Hope and Ruby, her Wirehaired Fox Terrier puppy;
Milo and Snoop, his Welsh Terrier puppy;
Tony and Rocco, his Jack Russell cross puppy.

Models
Amber, Jasmine, Benetta, Milo, Charlie, and Joe